Aug. 2024

Hope you ......
these ......
stories ......
Australia.

x Diana &
  Ron

CW00420006

GURAWUL

THE WHALE

This is a Magabala Book

LEADING PUBLISHER OF ABORIGINAL AND TORRES STRAIT ISLAND STORYTELLERS.

CHANGING THE WORLD, ONE STORY AT A TIME.

First published 2023

Magabala Books Aboriginal Corporation
1 Bagot Street, Broome, Western Australia
Website: www.magabala.com
Email: sales@magabala.com

Magabala Books receives financial assistance from the Commonwealth Government through the Australia Council, its arts advisory body. The State of Western Australia has made an investment in this project through the Department of Local Government, Sport and Cultural Industries. Magabala Books would like to acknowledge the generous support of the Shire of Broome, Western Australia.

Magabala Books is Australia's only independent Aboriginal and Torres Strait Islander publishing house. Magabala Books acknowledges the Traditional Owners of the Country on which we live and work. We recognise the unbroken connection to the traditional lands, waters and cultures. Through what we publish, we honour all our Elders, peoples and stories, past, present and future.

Cover and internal design by Emilia Toia
Black-and-white illustrations by Laura La Rosa
Printed in China by Everbest Printing Company

ISBN Print 978-1-922613-89-9
ISBN ePDF 978-1-922613-90-5

A catalogue record for this book is available from the National Library of Australia

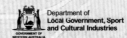

An ancient story for our time

GURAWUL
THE WHALE

MAX DULUMUNMUN HARRISON

Illustrations Laura La Rosa

Magabala
BOOKS

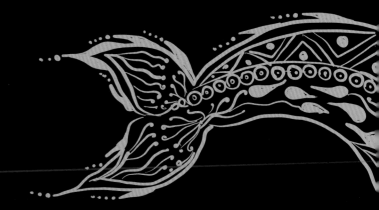

CONTENTS

Foreword   06

Preface   08

The Promise   16

1   From Land to Sea: Gurawul's Story   20

2   My Journey with Gurawul Begins   32

3   Singing Up the Whales   44

4   Keeping the Promise   58

5   Handing Down the Legacy   74

Acknowledgements and Notes   92

The Author   94

The Illustrator   95

FOREWORD

I acknowledge Uncle Max Harrison, minga Dulumunmun, for the teachings we have come through and hold. The teachings of Gurawul are important to this country and the world. Gurawul teaches us about the best way for us to live, how to be resilient, how to hold responsibility for looking after country. Gurawul is now on its annual journey; a journey that is ancient, with no starting time and hopefully no end time. As it swims from cold country to warm country, it's looking after country all the way, singing country. It teaches its young ones about the places to be, to rest, to eat, and the places to stay away from.

Uncle Max would want us to continue what he taught us about looking after Gurawul, because our story is about Gurawul being on the land with us and asking the old people for permission to go to the sea, to look after the foods, medicines and important places that are sea country. When Gurawul comes back to the land, it's not always because of radar and sonar. It's coming back because it's holding its lore, its responsibility. It's giving up its life as it promised the old people, bringing back the lore That is the time to come together, to feed and celebrate, but also a time to remember our responsibility for country.

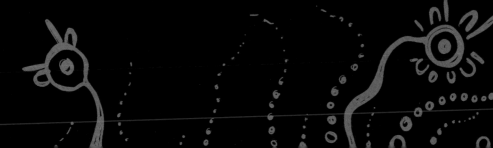

Uncle Max was my teacher, uncle and friend. He was so humble in his way of teaching that it allowed anyone to learn. He always talked about nature and what his old teachers taught him about nature. He used to say nature is the greatest teacher, the biggest classroom and the largest university. We spent many times together and I learned so much from that old man. Uncle Max is still with us even though he's physically gone. His suitcase has gone back into the ground, the mother, but his spirit is ever present, and every time I try to take a short cut that old man reminds me: don't take the short cut, go the long road and then you'll learn the basic lessons of respect, patience and tolerance. We can learn if we watch, hear and feel what is in front of us. We do that one day at a time because we can only live one day at a time and always stay in the present.

Uncle Max is with me in spirit for the rest of my life. *Natcha tung nunga, through the mother, Mother Earth.*

Dean Kelly

PREFACE

It is an honour to be writing these words for this book from the man I held so close and dear, my grandfather Max. I was privileged to be with him at most of the places where he received the pieces of this epic landscape puzzle. I met the people and was privy to the trials and tribulations of his quest, chasing a story first sketched on a dusty road in the Bega Valley hinterlands. We would both marvel and gasp with a quick glance at each other when the next layer of the story revealed itself. These were monumental and powerful moments for not just us, but all who were close to him.

On 11 December 2021, Uncle Max made his transition to the sky country. He now sits alongside and among the wisdom of the Ancestors since writing this book.

'Follow the bubbles, I will show you the way' is now a mantra for us collectively. This dreaming story is one for the ages. Myself, our bloodline and others under his teachings all bask in the array of lessons and sheer abundance of the old ways he handed down. I hope you too can embrace and absorb the legacy, the story and the spirit of Uncle Max following Gurawul the Whale.

Through the mother.

Dwayne Bannon-Harrison, 2022

Gurawul binji moonyip

Whale pregnant travelling

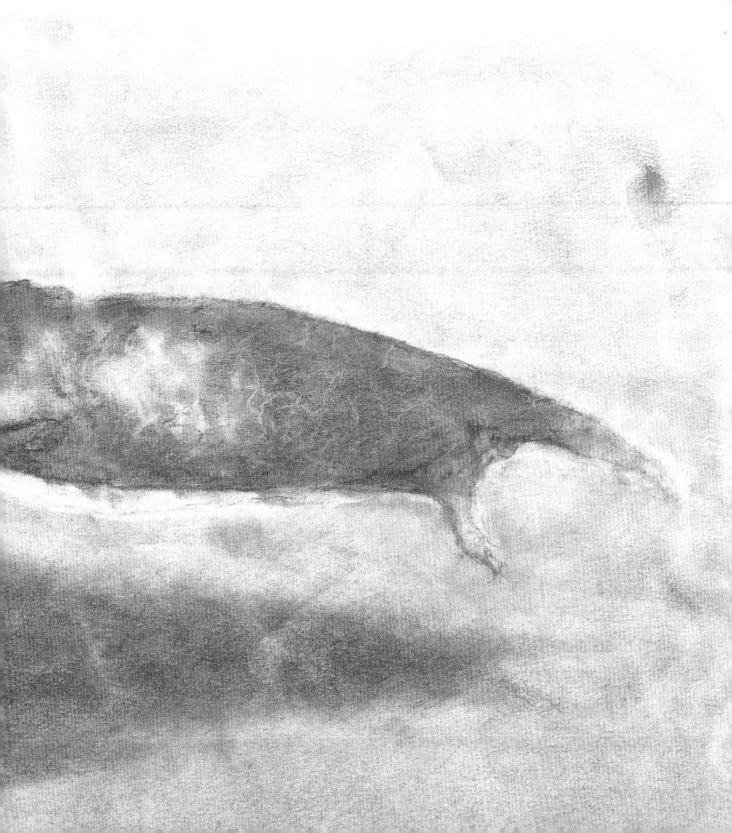

Gurawul boorai moonyip

Whale with child travelling

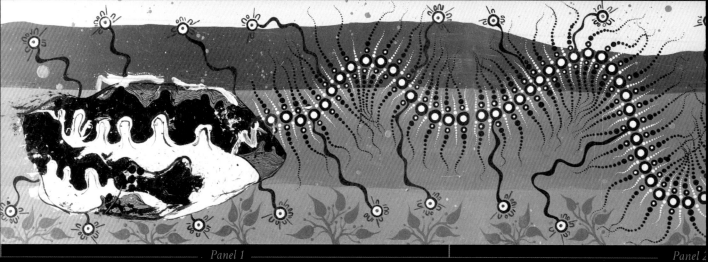

This painting was first designed in Photoshop by Wayne Thorpe after returning from a visit to Tasmania with Uncle Max. The rocks there have engravings carved in them depicting the Gurawul story that was handed to Uncle Max by his grandfather and uncles when he was 10 years old.

During the 2021 ceremony camp at Brogo, Wayne showed the Gurandji the Photoshop image, to let the artists Peter Hewitt, Brendan Lugnan and Jeremy Devitt paint the design of the Gurawul dreaming story.

Each artist painted a panel of the story, completing it at the ceremony camp. When they showed Uncle Max, he cried as he remembered his old masters who taught him the story. The artists said to him: 'This painting is for you, Uncle, please do not sell it. It's for you to keep and remember the dreaming story.' Uncle Max agreed that it is priceless because it has recorded his memory of the dreaming story of the Ancestors following the bubbles of Gurawul the whale.

The three panels were then framed together and digitally joined.

Panel 1 depicts the rock of carvings of confused faces. The confusion and chaos was caused by the flooding waters as ice melted after the last Ice Age.

Panel 2 depicts the bubbles left by the whales as they showed the people the way, to follow them from east to west to higher ground and then across the land bridge from what is now Tasmania to what is now mainland Australia. Each of the circles attached to the line of bubbles represents one of the senior men at the ceremony camp.

Panel 3 depicts Gurawul the whale migrating from the Antarctic to Kari – Hervey Bay – each year, as they pass by each of the language groups along the way and back again to the Antarctic with their young offspring.

Wayne Thorpe, *Senior Lore Man*

Panel 3

'This painting is for you,
Uncle, to keep and remember
the dreaming story.'

THE
PROMISE

All my life, for as long as I can remember, I have been following the teachings of my Elders and singing up Gurawul the whale. Along the beaches, we sing up and dance the return of Gurawul, celebrating the lore and medicines this sacred being offers to share with us, providing us with food and helping to restore peace in our land.

When I was 10 years old, I was given Gurawul's story by my grandfather Muns and three old uncles. On the ground, in the dirt, they drew the whale dreaming story and asked me to make a promise: to go to the southern land and search for the whale dreaming passed on by the Ancestors. When I made that promise, I had no idea what it meant or that it would take me 70 years to keep it.

Here then is Gurawul's story as I first heard it, as it has been passed down through the ages from the Ancestors, and the story of how I kept my promise.

When I was 10 years old,
I was given Gurawul's story by
my grandfather Muns and
three old uncles.

Chapter 1

FROM LAND TO SEA:
GURAWUL'S STORY

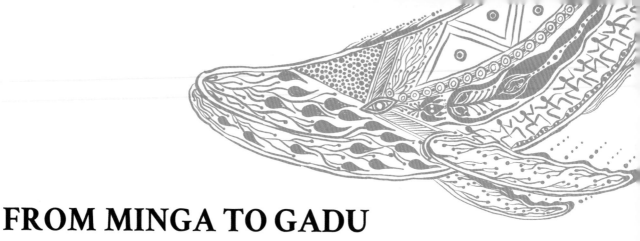

FROM MINGA TO GADU

Many millions of years ago, long before they swam in the ocean, whales lived on Minga (the land). Looking out to the oceans, they decided to ask the Elders for permission to go into Gadu (the ocean), to look after the fish and all the other creatures living there.

'You people can look after the foods and medicines on dry land,' the whales said. 'We need to get back into Gadu to help look after the foods and medicines there.'

Up and down the coast and right across the country, a council of Elders was called.

'We will give you permission to go back into Gadu,' the Elders said, 'and look after the food and medicines. But there is one important thing we need you to do. We need you to come and give yourself back to the people to share the lore.'

There was one other promise that the Elders asked the whales to keep, which was to follow the dreaming track off the Continental Shelf as they were heading north. That way, our people could track them from headland to headland and catch the fish that followed them.

SHARING THE LORE

The whales agreed to return and give themselves back to the people by beaching themselves onto the shore. Sometimes the whales would come in numbers, but usually a solitary whale was the one that brought the lore of the sea.

As soon as someone saw the whale on the beach, an Elder was called to ceremoniously spear the whale. The spear was pushed down and the whale turned over, belly up, to regurgitate the lore. The spear would be pulled back out without breaking it, and the message was sent out to all the nations from far and wide to come together to feast and hold corroboree. The rest of the men would pull the whale over and put it belly up, facing the heavens. This would allow the spirit of the whale to leave the body and for the lore to be regurgitated.

Imagine a beautiful beach that you're standing upon and looking along its shores. Imagine one of those great mammals coming into the shores. Hearing the noise they make, communicating with some of the Elders on the shore.

I have three ancient spears that have been passed on to me: one is for spearing fish, another for hand-to-hand combat. The other spear is made from a hard sturdy wood and is for Gurawul.

The message was sent out to all the nations far and wide to come together to feast and hold a corroboree. All the different clans and mobs would arrive to feast on the whale that had given its life so the lore could be known. While the people were eating the flesh of the whale, they would be learning more of the wisdom of the ocean and the land and sharing and caring with each other what they were feasting on, passing the lore on to other clan groups.

For days and weeks the great gathering would continue. The food was always divided equally; everyone knew that this part was this tribe's food and that part was that tribe's food. When it was over, different tribes would take a big slice of whale meat away and bury it. If a whale didn't come for a while, they could bring the food back and unite together again to do their feasting.

This was an important ritual to restore peace in the land. There were no wars or fighting. Gurawul gave up its life and its body so that people would unite.

WHALE
MIGRATION
in Australia

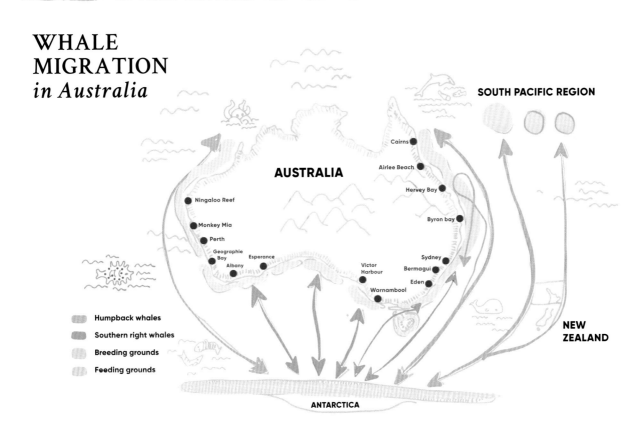

SOUTH PACIFIC REGION

AUSTRALIA

Cairns

Airlee Beach

Hervey Bay

Ningaloo Reef

Byron bay

Monkey Mia

Perth

Geographie
Bay
Albany

Esperance

Sydney

Victor
Harbour

Bermagui

Eden

Warnambool

**NEW
ZEALAND**

Humpback whales

Southern right whales

Breeding grounds

Feeding grounds

ANTARCTICA

The humpback whale migrates huge distances – up to 25,000 km – between polar regions in summer, and tropical or subtropical waters in winter. After feeding in the Antarctic waters in summer, in June to August Australian humpbacks begin their migration up the western and eastern coast of Australia to their breeding grounds close to shore. The southern right whale also spends its summers in the feeding grounds around Antarctica, then migrates to the south and eastern coastlines of Australia to breed.

HOW THE WHALES LED THE PEOPLE TO SAFETY

At the end of the last Ice Age, about 12,000 years ago, the glaciers thawed and melted and the sea level rose. The Bassian Plain disappeared under water, closing the pathways into the southernmost region of the continent. The people living in the southern part of the land were afraid of drowning. They were upset and confused about what to do as the water started to rise and flood their hunting grounds and campsites. Thousands of square kilometres were covered by the water. The whales could feel the water level rising and used every method they could to alert people to the danger. They told them not to worry, they would show them where to go. 'And what if we get lost?' the people asked. 'Can we make it?' 'Follow us and we'll lead you to safety,' the whales said. 'Follow our bubbles and we'll lead you to higher ground.'

They started blowing through their blowholes and grinding (letting their bubbles go) so that the tribes could follow them. It was their way of leaving a trail, like walking through the bush and bending a twig. They couldn't leave those marks on the water, so they blew their bubbles for the people to follow.

BUBBLE *netting*

Humpback whales use an unusual hunting method called 'bubble netting'. A group of whales works together, swimming in a circle around a school of krill, all the while blowing bubbles from their blowholes, directing their prey into the centre of their 'net'.

At that time, Tasmania was a big mountain. Rising water submerged the flat lands, which became Bass Strait, cutting Tasmania off from the mainland. This isolated the people there from the rest of humankind for several thousand years – the longest isolation of any human group in history. The tribal groups who had lived on the flat lands looked after many sacred and significant sites. In recent times, this is where oil and gas have been discovered. Some of the tribes came across to the mainland and stayed there, where they still are today. Some of them kept walking up the Continental Shelf along the eastern seaboard into southern New South Wales and Victoria. Others went through the Great Australian Bight and up the west coast.

Some people say we came out of Africa, but we say we followed the whale from the south — Gurawul.

WAYNE THORPE

Other people stayed in Tasmania, moving up onto higher ground. Once they reached a place of safety, they wanted to find a way to express their gratitude to the whales and to record what had happened. After finding the shape of Gurawul in a rock, they carved their faces of confusion and fear onto a large flat rock. Then, over the rocks in a wave-like pattern, they engraved the whales' bubbles that led them to safety.

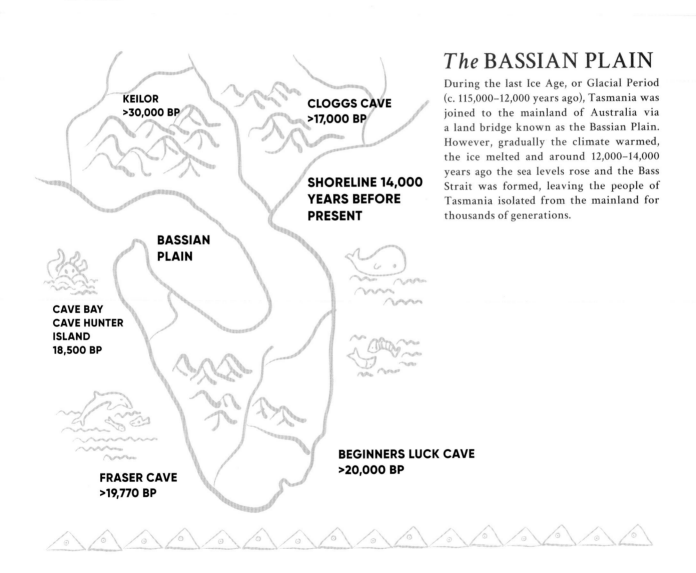

KEILOR
>30,000 BP

CLOGGS CAVE
>17,000 BP

SHORELINE 14,000
YEARS BEFORE
PRESENT

BASSIAN
PLAIN

CAVE BAY
CAVE HUNTER
ISLAND
18,500 BP

BEGINNERS LUCK CAVE
>20,000 BP

FRASER CAVE
>19,770 BP

The BASSIAN PLAIN

During the last Ice Age, or Glacial Period (c. 115,000–12,000 years ago), Tasmania was joined to the mainland of Australia via a land bridge known as the Bassian Plain. However, gradually the climate warmed, the ice melted and around 12,000–14,000 years ago the sea levels rose and the Bass Strait was formed, leaving the people of Tasmania isolated from the mainland for thousands of generations.

SCIENCE AND *the* LEGENDS

Science is starting to show there's some truth in these 'old blackfella' stories. Scientists are now discovering that the ancestors of whales once lived on land. My old scientists said the same thing! The first whales evolved over 50 million years ago. I can go all the way back to when the whales asked permission to go into Gadu and came down from the mountains through the waterholes, streams and rivers. I believe Gurawul's story proves that we did not walk from Africa, it precedes this migration story, and we're continuing to find sites that precede it by thousands of years.

The EVOLUTION OF *the whale*

The first 'whales', or cetacean mammals, evolved in the Early Eocene Epoch around 50 million years ago. One of these ancient whales, Pakicetus, was a carnivorous, wolf-like land animal with functional legs, which lived near freshwater sources and ate mainly fish. The cetaceans' transition from land to sea occurred approximately 49 million years ago. Ambulocetus natans (the 'running whale'), which lived at that time, was amphibious and still had legs, but its mobility on land was limited. By the late Eocene, cetaceans such as Dorudon began to resemble modern whales. They no longer had legs and they lived in fully marine habitats. Interestingly, the closest (non-cetacean) living relative of the modern whale is the hippopotamus.

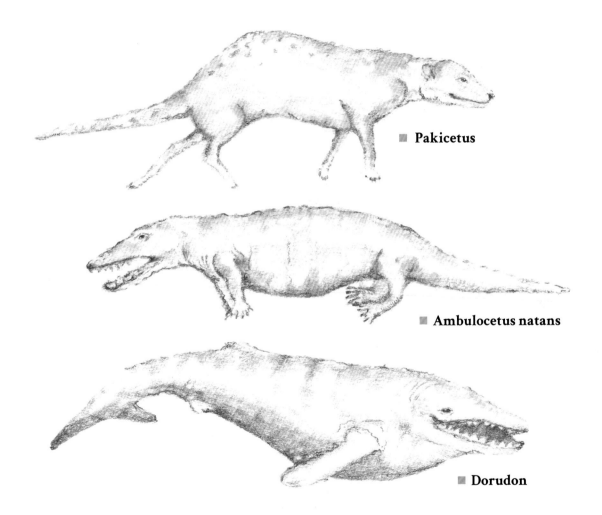

■ Pakicetus

■ Ambulocetus natans

■ Dorudon

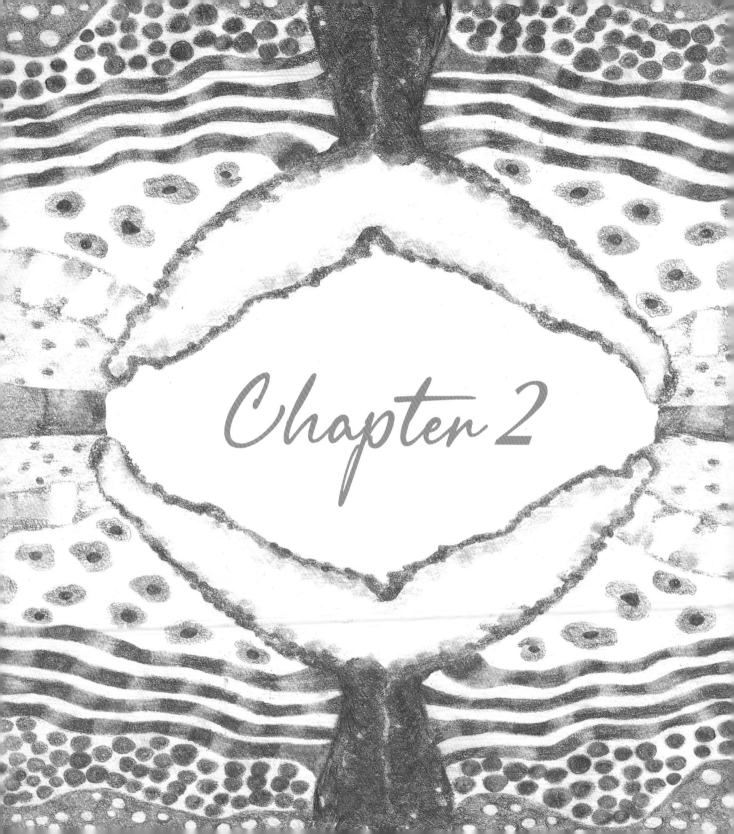

Chapter 2

MY JOURNEY

WITH GURAWUL BEGINS

WALKING TO CATHCART

Growing up, my family consisted of Mum Agnes, her sister Mum Vera, their uncle, Grandfather Muns, and all my brothers and sisters and cousins. The men were away working, usually either logging or in the sawmill. We would travel together in a group, moving around from New South Wales to Victoria and back again. When I was around four or five, we decided it was time to leave Bega. Playing ping pong with the Welfare, we moved across to Orbost in Victoria where we were safer.

In 1947, the year my youngest sister Calita was born on the banks of the Snowy River, we moved back to Bega, where there was field work picking beans and peas. Even though I loved the Snowy River, when it was time to move you had to 'pack up your troubles in your old kit bag and smile, smile, smile!' The soldiers used to sing that song and that's what they'd sing to us young ones every time we had to move, to keep the morale up. 'You mean the old sugar bag?' someone would ask – because that's what we used for suitcases!

Mum, Mum Vera and my sisters, along with the younger ones, left Orbost in a truck to go back to Bega and on to Wallaga Lake but there wasn't enough room for me.

'He'll be right,' said Grandfather Muns. 'He can walk with us and get the teachings.' And so began my teaching journey, walking with Grandfather, Uncle Hugo, Uncle Weenie One and Uncle Chok.

For the first 10 miles I felt a bit sad, not because I couldn't go with Mum and the others but because they were missing out on the teachings that I was going to be getting. As we walked, finding stones and different plants, vines and fruit, I learned about privileges, tolerance and acceptance. At the time I thought, if I get bold and get hit with the *bundi* (stick), my memory won't retain all this wonderful stuff. Then I also thought, I'll have this to be able to pass down, and I was pretty joyful about that.

Every day when I woke up until I closed my eyes at night, it was lessons and teachings. I learned to live just for today and to fill my sunrise to sunset taking in information, accepting it and not questioning it. I had to really hold those stories.

Sometimes when we sat down, I'd notice how Grandfather and the uncles sat in position, waving me into a spot with a gesture of the hand. I could feel where I had to sit and put myself where I was looking at their faces. At night listening to the stories around the flickering flames of the campfire, I could see the shadows of their faces. Sometimes when I'm talking about them, I can still see their faces in the firelight.

A STORY I NEVER FORGOT

When we got to a little place called Cathcart in the Southern Tablelands, there was a fork in the dirt road. One way led down Mount Darragh, the other down Tantawangalo Mountain. Both mountains are significant dreaming tracks. Uncle Hugo picked up a stick as Grandfather started to speak.

'We'll tell you a story you'll never forget!' he said, and with those powerful words he handed down to me the story of Gurawul the whale. Straight away, I knew this story was an important part of our journey.

As Grandfather was telling me Gurawul's story, I watched Uncle Hugo drawing circles in the dirt. I can still see him now, his shoulder in line with the mountain range behind him. Some of the marks were rings while some had a line or two through them. Then there was another one he drew, a circle with a lot of scribbly marks inside it. 'You've got to look for these patterns, go and look for these faces,' Grandfather said, adding, 'These are the bubbles of the whale. Follow them and then you'll see the whale.'

Grandfather made me promise that one day I would go and find the patterns in a foreign country that he and the old uncles had never been to and I didn't even know about, a place called Tasmania.

'Yeah, okay Pop, okay Uncle,' I said, nodding my head in agreement because I wanted to keep this promise. Perhaps I was frightened of getting the *bundi* or something; I guess I was agreeing out of fear, because I didn't know if I could keep the promise, especially at that age.

When Grandfather and the uncles told me stories, I had to shut up and couldn't ask questions. I'd been told something and asking questions would be disrespectful. If your mind was ahead of the story, they'd say, 'Well, you know … so we won't tell you!' When they were ready, they would come back to the story. This is the old fellas' way of teaching.

Grandfather put his old black foot over the markings and rubbed them out. When he did that I felt devastated but I knew the promise had to be kept. I made up my mind that I'd have to find them.

What I didn't know was that it would take me 70 years before I could fulfil my promise.

Beware of THE BUNYIP

As kids, the old people told us the story of the bunyip to put fear into us, to keep us out of waterholes if no one was there to look after us. Waterholes were pretty muddy and murky and the mud was so deep, kids could get caught in there and no one would hear you singing out. A form of discipline, it frightened the living daylights out of us.

Mum and Mum Vera always told us to stay away from the swamp near Snaggers Lane. 'If you go into that waterhole,' they said, 'the bunyip will grab you.' Even though we were told not to go there, my sisters and I sometimes went anyway. Next to the swamp was a walnut tree and we used to gather the nuts that had fallen on the ground. One day we were picking up the nuts when we looked up and, right in front of us, we saw a cow being pulled into the swamp and disappearing ... just like that! Dropping the nuts, we ran back home like hell and told Mum about seeing the cow disappear.

'What were you doing near the swamp?' she asked. 'Getting walnuts,' we said. 'Where are the walnuts?' she asked. 'Brother chucked 'em,' my sisters said, pointing at me.

Mum might have believed us if I hadn't thrown them away, but unfortunately I had, so we got whacked with the big stick for being disobedient. Poor little brother got the first hit, then my sisters.

Just down from Orbost is a little place called Marlo. The old people used to talk about how the bunyip goes down to Marlo to feed on salt in the salt water before coming back up to two waterholes. We always wanted to go and swim in them but we weren't allowed; we had to go and swim in the river instead. When the snow melted up in the mountains around Jindabyne, the Orbost flats would be flooded and the waterholes would fill with the overflow.

'But didn't the bunyip get washed away?' we used to ask. 'No,' the old people said. 'They knew how to stay in strong water.'

There were times when I could have questioned them but that was the big no-no. If I started asking questions, they'd say, 'Just shut your mouth, Max! Zip your lips and open your mind!'

'Remember the waterholes over there at Orbost?' Grandfather Muns asked. 'We told you to keep away from the waterholes because of that bunyip? We think that that fella *dunga* (the bunyip) is Gurawul.'

There's no proof that the bunyip was Gurawul but, even when we do have scientific confirmation of legends, we still have to keep the legends alive because they reveal and explain creation. The old people were closer to nature than the scientists. And so I respect the story of the bunyip.

WAS DIPROTODON *the bunyip?*

Fossilised skeletons of an enormous wombat-like creature from the Pleistocene Epoch (2.6 million–11,700 years ago) have been unearthed in Australian dry salt lakes. About 1.8 metres in height and weighing about 3 tonnes, Diprotodon was the largest marsupial in history and may have lurked in swamps while looking for prey.

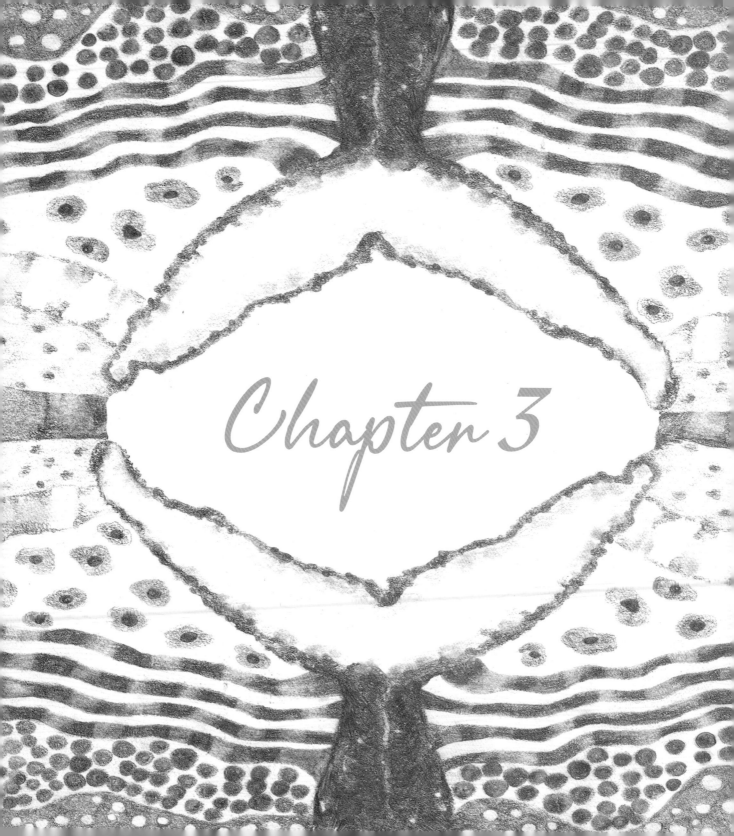

Chapter 3

SINGING

UP THE WHALES

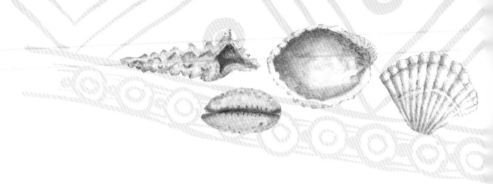

A WINK FROM GURAWUL

Once, when I was 16, a whale washed up at Bermagui. While people were getting ropes and boats and a tractor to pull it back out to sea, I went down to have a closer look at this wonderful creature and while I was looking at the eye, the eye winked at me. That was when I knew I had to continue my journey and keep telling the story of Gurawul the whale. Around Bega and Wallaga, people talked about bunyips in the waterholes, so I would talk about the belief I had that somehow the bunyip was Gurawul the whale. It had once been on land and now it was this beautiful creature in the ocean.

Everywhere I went up and down the coast, I started to tell little stories about Gurawul the whale, not realising that I had a big story to tell. I was ridiculed by the scientists when I told them that they beached themselves because of their promise to all the tribes and past Elders. At times I felt like some old blackfella with this Dreamtime story but I

kept the story going. Then I thought, I'm talking about this wonderful creature but what am I doing about it?

I took whatever chances I could. I started taking people whale watching in Jervis Bay and as we went out, I'd rub my hands with glee while I sang up Gurawul. It started to terrify the people because the whales were coming up alright! Right beside the boat and underneath. The tour operators were saying, 'That was close!' I thought I'd better shut my mouth.

With the rising of Grandmother Moon
and the setting of Grandmother Moon

and with the rising of Grandfather Sun
and the setting of Grandfather Sun

Those two spiritual Ancestors help us, guide us,
to understand the movement
of Gurawul the whale

UNCLE MAX'S WORDS BEFORE THE WHALE CEREMONY WHEN
BOTH THE MOON AND SUN CAN BE SEEN IN THE SKY

THE WHALE CEREMONY

Singing up the whales on their journey is about nurturing the pregnant mother all the way up to the nursery near Fraser Island on the east coast and then bringing the mother and baby back safely. Performing the Gurawul ceremony creates a connection between those taking part in the ceremony and Gurawul. I do the ceremony because of the spiritual connection that I have with this wonderful being, for its protection and letting it move on its journey.

My instructions were to continue my ceremony and let our people know that this is the movement and the ceremony that we should be doing every year to give the whales a safe journey going up and coming back. When we're singing them up, we're singing them up so that they show themselves to let us know that they're okay. We are trying to be the unofficial protectors of the whale.

The last time we did the ceremony, out near Kurnell, there were about 40 people doing the movement so Gurawul could show and let us know they were travelling safe. Just as we finished the dance, four whales breached. That is the spiritual connectedness that I talk about, which I must keep teaching people to hold this long tradition. There is no ceremony which is complete and ends, it is a continuous process of doing ceremonies. The land talks to us and when we see the beautiful golden wattle, we know that these whales are going north to have their babies. That's why we sing them on that safe journey. There are so many elements to the ceremony and the more you try to separate it, the more you find other things. When people go through lore they discover all the different layers.

SACRED DANCE AND SONG

The dance has always been done, way back to the ancients. When I was being taught it, I'd hear the clapping sticks being thrown to the ground and that's when I knew I was making mistakes. I'd think, 'Oh geez, I don't want that around my legs'. Then when I heard the clapping of the sticks again, I felt I was doing the dance and singing the song right. It's only a short song but, still, it has been so important for me to hold that song for that large being. It is a huge responsibility.

The movement of the ceremonial dance is the same movement that the whale does when it's travelling up the eastern seaboard. It comes from the South Pole into the Great Australian Bight, around the bottom then up and around Fraser Island, where it comes in from the reef and into the bay to birth. Coming back it moves a little further out into the ocean, following a figure-eight movement.

In the dance, there are two parts. In the first part, we sing *Gurawul binji moonyip* while the dancers take their position in the shape of the whale. One flipper goes up, the other one goes down and the tail at the back goes up and down. When the head goes down, they all bend down before rising up again, creating a beautiful movement. When the whales are coming back, we sing about the baby that has now been birthed, with the words *Gurawul boorai moonyip.*

When a film crew wanted to make a film about the whales, I called seven or eight of the fellas together and got them to practise the dance.

'No phones, no cameras, nothing,' I told the crew. That was the condition I made if they wanted to see this sacred dance, singing the whales up, being performed. They kept their promise and stood there respectfully.

'You've witnessed this sacred dance and song,' I said. 'In the morning we'll go out and see what comes.'

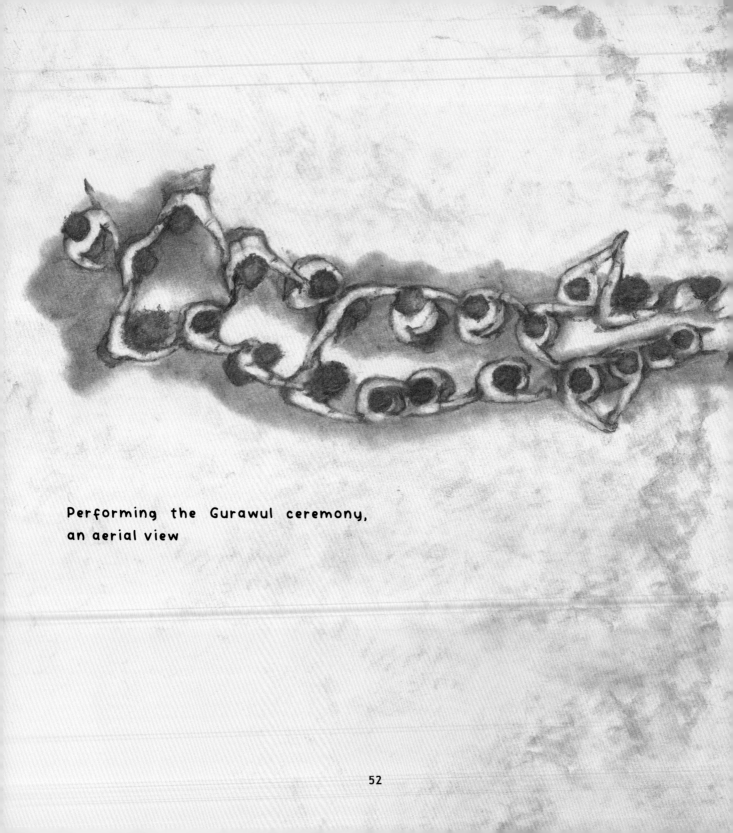

Performing the Gurawul ceremony,
an aerial view

I'm here to respect the ancestor of the sea, *Gurawul the whale,* and to send him and the family, the mothers, the babies and that family of whales home to their country, where they come from – the cold waters. So we sung them up to do that and help them on their journey. It's what we have to do.

DEAN KELLY

The next morning at six o'clock, we went out in a small boat just north of Barranguba. Seagulls were flying overhead while seals and dolphins played in the water.

'Look what's coming,' I said. 'Just seals and dolphins,' they said. 'Yeah,' I said. 'But why are they there? They're going to enjoy the krill that's being pushed down this way.'

Suddenly, the whales were everywhere. They came around the boat and under it, doing figure-eights. Sometimes we thought one of the big fellas was going to hit us. Sitting up the top, the skipper's jaw dropped. In over 10 years of whale watching, he'd never seen them come up like this – there were over 300 of them!

'How did you do that!?' he asked. 'Better ask Uncle Max,' someone said.

It wasn't so much me singing them up – I haven't got the power – but they needed the words to come up. When I think about singing Gurawul up, it's no fluke, no miracle. It just happens.

When Gurawul's eye winked at me on the beach at Bermagui, it gave me the courage to keep going, to keep Gurawul's story alive. The last time I was down that way, all the babies were coming back and they were so close. I've never seen that before.

Talk it up, sing it up!

Today was about the promise. About the story of creation that stems way back. And it's an honour to be in this space, doing, practising, living, breathing that story in 2020. It's an absolute honour to link it to what I call the universal highway. We all take little exits and entries and come off the universal highway but it binds us through humanity and all those universal lores and that ultimately comes back to the Mother Earth, Father Sky, the Grandmother Moon and Grandfather Sun, to connect to something deeper to us is so, so important. Ultimately it's about keeping the connection between salt water (Gadu) and the land (Minga), that connection, but also the stories that are here are also under there. Up on our creation mountain, Mother Gulaga, Gurawul is in there, etched in stone and breaching up to honour that old promise to the old people. And to be a part of that story, and continuing that song — the language and the movement — is something else.

DWAYNE BANNON-HARRISON, GRANDSON OF
MAX DULUMUNMUN HARRISON

RED DUST STORM

After the red dust storm came through Sydney in 2009, I saw the whales rising everywhere and thrashing. The only scientific reason I can see is that when all that red dust settled down into the ocean, the plankton came up and the whales were feasting on it.

When I look at the west coast, the red dirt is much closer and there's a lot of whale movement. Around Broome, before they go up into the nursery, they can feast with the little easterly wind because the red dirt is so close to the ocean.

When the dust storm happened, I was launching a friend's book in the city. Five or six Aboriginal aunties from the Red Centre were at the launch.

'So you've brought the red dust with you?' I said to them and we laughed. 'You can come again because you're feeding the whales.'

Everyone was worried about their shiny cars getting dirty and how much it took to get them clean. Nobody ever thought about the food it brought for Gurawul.

Chapter 4

KEEPING THE
PROMISE

GOING TO TASMANIA

Seventy years after Grandfather told me Gurawul's story and made me promise to find the engravings, I decided it was time to keep it. I could still remember the words he spoke to me when I was 10 years old.

'Remember what we said about going to find Gurawul the whale?' Grandfather had said. 'And looking for those circles?' He was talking about the circles Uncle Hugo had drawn in the dirt at Cathcart. I realised now that they represented the bubbles of the whale, and I knew I had to go to Tasmania and look for the engravings. They would be such an important part of Gurawul's story and our people's story.

There had been lots of reasons why I hadn't gone to Tasmania before then – family commitments, working during the sixties and seventies in the Snowy Mountains, different responsibilities.

At the end of 2015, just before Christmas, I received one of my spiritual emails, which I never ignore. I was talking about how I'd love to go down to Tasmania and see if I could find where Grandfather Muns and the uncles had spoken about.

'Let's do it,' my partner Marelle said. 'Let's go down.' She booked everything and a small group of us – Marelle, two of my granddaughters and me – drove from Sydney to Port Phillip Bay to catch the *Spirit of Tasmania* to Devonport. Before the boat sailed, I pulled out a bit of paper and a pen. From memory, I drew what Uncle Hugo had drawn in the dirt on the paper.

'I think this is what I've gotta find,' I said as I put the paper in my wallet and into my pocket. It felt like mission impossible!

As we sailed out of Melbourne, we found a spot up the front and laid back on the deckchairs. My head was like the clown at the fair looking for Gurawul – open-mouthed, looking from side to side.

In Hobart, we joined up with Jim Everett, a Pakana (Tasmanian) fella, who took us to Bruny Island. As well as Bruny Island, whaling stations were established in Tasmania at Recherche Bay, Southport, Spring Bay, Maria Island, Freycinet Peninsula, Forestier Peninsula and Bicheno.

Whaling began in Tasmania with the beginnings of white colonisation. The early white colonists of Tasmania observed large numbers of the southern right whale migrating from the cold southern waters up towards the coast of eastern Australia to breed. They set up a whaling industry in order to hunt the whales for their valuable oil and blubber.

Whale oil was used in Britain for street lighting and industrial processes, and whale bone from 'baleen' whales was stitched into women's dresses. Large numbers of southern right whales came into the bays and inlets along the coast during their annual migration north from Antarctica. In the 1830s, about 3000 southern right whales were killed. The whale population was in decline by the late 1870s and '80s due to indiscriminate killing, and the last Tasmanian-based whaling voyage was in 1900.

On the beaches, we found a lot of whale bones. Around Adventure Bay, people had placed them in their yards and on their fences. It felt disrespectful and beyond my acceptance. Then I thought, am I overlooking one of the wonderful teachings from my ancients about acceptance of events, acceptance of past and present? I knew that I had to heal and continue keeping the stories alive, just as when the ancients were caring for the whales. Giving it away to keep … that's an important thing that they taught me. I must give it away to keep. I must give this story away so that I can keep my sanity, keep my peace, and keep my respect for my fellow human beings and totems.

We were there for about two or three days, looking at rocks, but all I could find were three rings engraved into the rocks right next to the ocean. I thought, this can't be what I'm looking for. I felt there had to be more.

AUNTY GLORIA

In three more days, we were due to go back to the mainland and I was starting to give up hope when Jim told me about a Palawa woman who was the custodian of a site where there were engravings.

'Uncle Max,' he said, 'do you know Aunty Gloria?' 'No, I don't,' I answered. 'Well,' he said, 'Aunty Gloria lives up the east coast at a place called St Helens.' 'That's where we're going tomorrow,' I said, thinking to myself, this is how Spirit works.

Jim rang her up and after having a chat, he handed the phone to me. 'Jim's telling me you know where there are some engravings,' I said to her. 'Yes, I do,' she said. 'I can take you and show you.' Then she added, 'Can I take my granddaughter with me?'

'Aunty Gloria,' I said, 'you don't have to ask me that. You know where these sites and engravings are. This is your country, not mine.' For 44 years, she had been looking after the site without even knowing what the engravings meant.

FINDING GURAWUL

In January 2016, just before my 80th birthday, a small group of us drove to a mountain outside St Helens. It was a warm day, clear and bright. We knew we were going somewhere sacred so before heading up the mountain, we did a smoking ceremony and put on red headbands.

I didn't know what I was going to find but after feeling a sense of defeat on Bruny, I now felt more hopeful. Something about the synchronicity of being in St Helens and meeting Aunty Gloria gave me a sense that this might be the place.

As we were walking up, I didn't have to say anything. We knew to be quiet. Aunty Gloria led the way with her walking stick and I had my walking stick, the two of us motoring along. Once we got to the site, I headed over in the direction she indicated and found a big rock with all these etchings on it. We went a bit further and she pointed to all these rings engraved into the rocks, going up, going down, like a centipede.

'Oh my god,' I said. 'This is what I'm looking for!' 'Wait till you see the rest of them,' she said.

Once I saw the circles, I knew I had found what I was looking for. I went straight back to the rock with the etchings and jumped onto it, looking

around like a puppy dog. I still didn't really know what it was until I saw a face – a face of confusion.

'Aunty Gloria,' I said, 'where's the whale?' 'I don't know,' she said. 'Could be up over there somewhere. Have a look at those other ones … it could be in there.'

Climbing up over the rocks, I looked up and saw a big rock in the shape of a whale looking straight at me! 'Oh my god,' I said. 'There you are! You're not an engraving, you're the image.'

Grandfather and the uncles had told me that the engravings were running from east to west. I asked Aunty Gloria which way they ran. 'They run dead east–west,' she said.

'My grandfather told me that,' I replied. 'And the beauty of it was he was never down here.'

Now I had confirmation of the ancient story Grandfather Muns and the uncles had told me at Cathcart. Being able to find those etchings and rings meant the Dreamtime story had become a reality!

Since that first visit, I've been down to Tasmania five times. I can't let the story go.

In 2017, I took my grandson and some of the other young men I've been teaching to the site. Without me telling them, they figured out that the engravings were bubbles.

We took a photo of the rock of confusion and that night we put it up on a screen. You could see the faces of all the people in the etchings: some confused, some afraid, a mixture of expressions.

Being able to follow my grandfather's story all the way through to that discovery was so important for me. Grandfather and those old fellas couldn't dream that story up. It had to be related to them. That was the legacy he handed down and I'm continuing to hand it down.

Knowing and showing and living legacies are such an important part of our storytelling.

Left: *Uncle Max with Aunty Gloria.*

Below: *Robyn Swanson, Uncle Max and Julie Gissing on the track.*

Opposite: *Rock showing the bubble engravings.*

Left: *Rock showing engraved faces of confusion.*

Below and opposite: *The whale rock.*

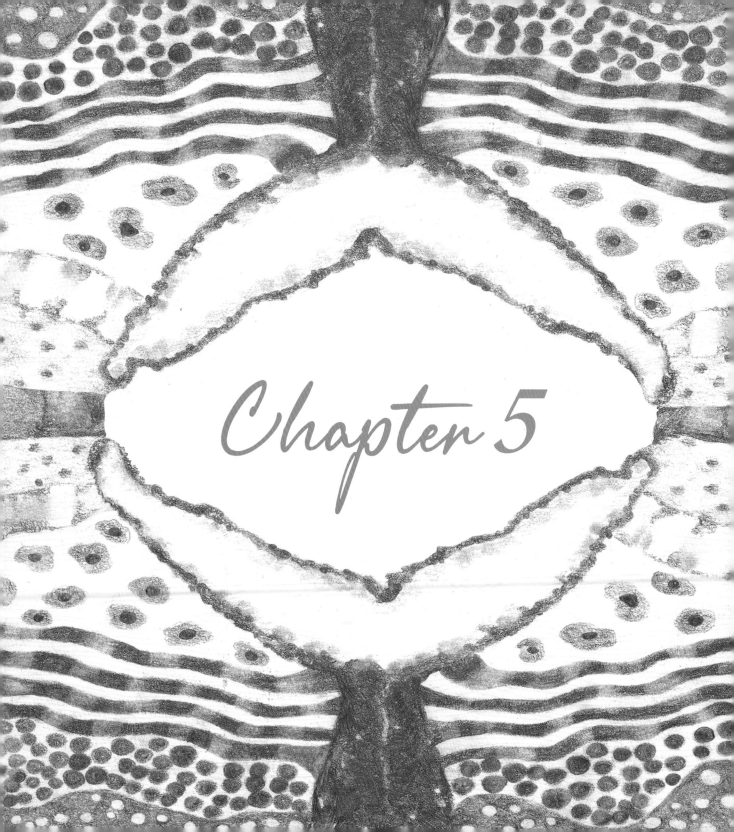

HANDING DOWN THE
LEGACY

FOLLOWING THE STORY

On my journeys up and down the east and west coast of Australia, I have been looking for people who might have had little bits of knowledge about Gurawul. One of our whale Elders up the top recently passed away. When Bunna Lawrie,[1] another whale fella in South Australia, informed me that now there were only two Elders left who held these stories about Gurawul, it took me aback.

A Noongar woman from Western Australia,[2] Alison Nannup, published a book called *Bindi-Bindi Koondarminy Wer Maamoong Waangka – Butterfly Dreaming and Whale Story*. In the book she tells the story about the whale regurgitating the lore when it came in to beach itself. I hardly hear anyone saying that, which was an important part of the story the old fellas told me in 1947.

When I was talking to Bunna Lawrie, he spoke about his grandfather who was a whale man, who also told me the story, possibly about the time he passed away in 1947. I know it's no coincidence, I know it's all spiritual connecting.

Nearly everyone around the coast has been talking about this wonderful being – I can't call it a creature, I've been calling it a being all these years – and what it's showing me is the connectedness that exists at all times. The humpback and the southern right are the two main whales I feel connected to.

The southern right whale used to spit out ambergris, which was sent to France to make perfume. It was pretty expensive stuff and the whales were slaughtered for it, with people getting rich. The Japanese have also hunted whales and devoured them for years. Our people also ate them – not too many people know that. I started to think if I could get the whales that have been beached and, instead of pulling them back out to sea, maybe we could do ceremony and then slice them up and send the meat to Japan. My head's in a mess thinking about all this – it's a big dilemma for me.

I remember that day when Gurawul got beached down at Bermagui. The authorities arrived and tried to pull it off the beach with trucks and bulldozers and trawlers, back out into the ocean. It still happens today if a whale beaches itself. But they forget about tidal movements and currents that will bring the whale straight back. I get so worked up when I think of it. Recently, they towed one out near the Royal National Park because they were frightened it would attract sharks while people were swimming. But they were swimming in the Figure Eight Pools, which are rock pools and the sharks can't get into those.

A SHARED STORY

It's been an important awakening for me to be travelling around and listening to a story that was told to me some 70-odd years ago. For a long time, the old people have been telling stories about these wonderful creatures that were originally on the land and how they wanted to go into the ocean, and what they did to get there – coming down the mountains through the waterholes, down the creeks, into the rivers and out into the ocean.

From Hervey Bay on the east coast and from the west coast in Western Australia, everywhere I went, the same story about the whale was told, indicating that all the tribal and language groups on the mainland shared it, although they gave the whale different names. Even in the language groups within the Yuin nation, I found some little changes in the name.

LANGUAGE NAMES *of the Whale Dreaming* *(east coast)*

Binna bill/Pin.ner. pil.ler	Palawa Kani
Kounterbuul	Gunditjmara
Baawang	Gunnai
Gurawul / Muriyira	Yuin
Dorroongun	Dunghutti (Kempsey)
Gooroodja	Gumbaynggirr (Coffs Harbour)
Bowi Yumbalayla	Bundjalung (Byron Bay)
Yallingbila	Qwandamooka
Mookga Mookga	Butchula

Sometimes parts of the stories are lost. Someone might get a part of a story but there's a missing link, then in will come a fabrication to fill in the gap. This is something I could never do to my old fellas. I could never ever try to fill in the gaps in Gurawul's story.

When I went across to Western Australia, I found the same story coming down the river from the mountains, towards Margaret River and down into the ocean. I heard stories about the whales and their journey north around the headland. A connecting cave runs underneath the headland about 20 or 30 kilometres towards Margaret River and sometimes people can see the whales going in.

While we were having lunch, whales were breaching off the coast. I saw how they communicated, passing each other by and moving out. Those coming back with the babies had to have more krill and they were communicating about feeding the little ones.

Up near Broome are some significant birthing places. The people up there call it the nursery. A good friend, an inland fella but a saltwater man (he's passed over now), told me that some of his people used the language of the whale up there in his country, up in the Kimberley, even today. There are a lot of stories about a songline that runs from Broome straight through to Uluru and across to the eastern seaboard. I always wanted to find it and then the old fella stood me right on it.

There was once a great inland sea in the desert and there are stories about the whale coming through underneath and up into the inland sea. The old people said there was a time when the ocean came in and pushed the land up, pushing and forming sandstone and all the ranges. You can see the crystals and the cracks where there was volcanic pushing.

The old fellas have lived and understood this for 80,000 years or longer. They could read the land with their scientific knowledge.

Travelling on the east coast, I asked some of the old people up in Hervey Bay about any whale stories they knew. One fella told a story about how the whale was being pursued and how it jumped down through all these waterholes and then out into Hervey Bay for safety.

I heard another story when I met up with an old friend in Nambucca. He and his wife were down on the beach at Marlo in Victoria, grabbing some abalone shells, when an old woman came over the sand dune. 'Don't you touch those shells,' she said. 'They're not for you to touch. You can take these pipi shells.' Then she told them a story about how the whale once lived on land and how, when it beached itself, everybody came in and feasted on it, all the tribes, and there were no arguments, no fights.

'You just told a part of my story from down home,' I told him. About five kilometres from Marlo was where my great-grandfather survived a massacre.

***

This is an old story. Older than everything. When the world was new, the lore was created, and the whale and the serpent looked out and saw the ocean.

I will look after the land because that is my home, but who will look after the ocean? said the serpent.

BRUCE PASCOE, 'WHALE AND SERPENT', *SALT: SELECTED STORIES AND ESSAYS*, 2019

DREAMTIME TO REALITY

When Grandfather Muns and the uncles told me Gurawul's story at Cathcart 70-odd years ago, I was too young to realise how it would affect my life. Being able to pass on that teaching and create a legacy has kept me busy for the last 40 years, and I have to continue sharing Gurawul's story because it reminds us of our ancient heritage. It connects us to those ancient times when Gurawul walked the land and came down through the rivers and waterholes into Gadu to look after the food and medicines there.

For 80,000 years and upwards, we walked on this land. We walked for our food, we had the nutritional knowledge of the superfoods and our food was our medicine. When the white people saw the skinny blackfellas walking around, they thought they'd better feed them and fatten them up. When we went through the massacres and missions, our way of life changed, our food changed. We were forced to eat Western food that was no good for our metabolism. It brought us sicknesses and took away our way of life.

Despite all that, elements of the living culture survived and I'm so proud of being a part of the tail end of that traditional era, experiencing that living lifestyle. I used to love how they cooked birds and fish … packed them in clay, stuck them in the ashes, tapped the clay and when it made a hard, sharp sound, it was cooked. When you lifted the fish or bird out and laid it down and cracked the clay, all the scales and feathers came off. All the innards ended up inside as a little ball as big as your fingernail. And if you cracked it right, you had two plates, one for you and one for me. The ancient technology.

It's a privilege, it's an honour to be part of this story, this memory. What I don't want is this culture and this lesson of the whale to be just a story. Remembering is a powerful thing, but living and being and doing and holding that is much stronger. And that way it will never die. It will be more than just a story.

RHETT BURRASTON

THE ROLE OF GURAWUL IN OUR CULTURE AND TRADITIONS

When we were kids we looked for whale blubber along the beach. Regurgitated by the whale, it was actually ambergris, an important ingredient for perfume. It was like looking for gold because it was so valuable. Every time we went onto the beaches, from May up until November when the whales were coming back, we used to look and ask, 'Did you leave us anything?'

We'd walk along the beaches, fishing and moving from one point to the other. Sometimes we followed the whales out, throwing our lines in the ocean. We always caught a fish when the whales were around. As soon as we saw them we knew, 'Yes, we're going to get something there!' We communicated the same as we do with the dolphin, slapping sticks on the water – they called it slapping water – to bring the fish in. When I was three or four I witnessed my dad and the uncles doing it. It was a wonderful thing for me to see.

The old fellas knew that as soon as those whales came, they brought food and medicines as promised. That was a very big statement for the whales to make: 'If you allow us to go back into the ocean, into Gadu, we will then provide and look after the foods and the medicines!' That was always an important part of caring and sharing in our cultural lore. You can sit with cultural lore and wonder why. Why is it that every time the whales come past we get this kind of fish? Why is it that all the different shellfish come up? That was the promise they made.

Gurawul's story tells us about migration, about our life when we walked the land and walked with nature, hunting and gathering. We had to follow up different parts of the land, just as Gurawul does in the water, going up the coast.

I've seen many whale engravings in the Sydney basin, from the ocean at Newcastle to the Blue Mountains, following the Wingecarribee River down at Robertson in the Southern Highlands. The river becomes a big boundary for the people of the Sydney basin.

The old people sat on sandstone for hours and hours engraving. You see more engravings of whales coming back south, which makes sense because they go up, give birth, then bring the babies back. A lot of those engravings go right into the Blue Mountains. I wonder how much of the canvas was destroyed when Sydney and Parramatta were built, the roads and the arteries. You have the biggest art gallery in the world and you don't realise it.

The old people sat there and watched which way their food and medicines were moving. Then they created drawings and etchings to show the direction the animals were travelling in. That's telling people, this is our supermarket. This is the way these foods will come towards us. We don't have to run after them, we can just set traps and get whatever we need. It wasn't mass killing; one animal was killed to eat.

The whale story was an important part in that learning. Sometimes you'll see a band around a whale's girth, down towards their tail or up close to their head. Those bands tell us that these are the Elders for the lore. Once they were important beings on land and they still play a part, even though they're in the ocean. When we keep using those parts of the stories in our ceremonies and dance, we are upholding our cultural lore.

Our lore is something that can't be changed, can never be changed. It's not like British law that can be changed with a stroke of the pen. We can't change our cultural lore because it is a living thing. Without it, our

We've always got to put Country first. We need to start to value our earth and air and sun and water and all the other wonderful things in creation, and understand where things come from [pointing to the sea], and where they're at today, and therefore where they could go.

GREG SMART

cultural traditions will pass away. It's important for people to know that we can still practise our cultural lore in every little thing we do, when we dance, make fire, clap sticks and make music.

KEEPING GURAWUL'S STORY ALIVE

What we're trying to teach our mob now is that the land owns us, we never owned the land. And, as a traditional custodian, my responsibility has been to keep Gurawul's story alive so that we can continue caring for this ancient sacred being who has taught us so much about harmony, respect, sharing and caring. Human beings have closed their minds to the sacredness of this magnificent being and caused it so much harm and pain. Where do we run, where do we go to for safety while the mind of the human is so destructive and wanton at times? I'll ask for Spirit and great creator Dharama to guide me, to help me through. I don't have to rely on your judgement, I only need to be allowed to speak my feelings and my truth, *natcha tung nunga*, through the Mother.

Acknowledgements

Thank you to my Elders, my grandfather and my uncles for the knowledge handed down to me. Thanks to my partner, Marelle, for her support and to my mother for her spirit and for being with me on my journey throughout.

I would like to thank Aunty Gloria Andrews for showing me the place where the engravings were done. I believe Spirit guided me to meet her when I travelled to Tasmania to look for them. She had looked after that particular site for 44 years without knowing what they meant. When I saw the confused faces, the whale's bubbles and the whale itself in the form of a rock, I was convinced. Thank you Aunty Gloria for helping me complete the story of Gurawul the whale.

I would like to acknowledge Bunna Lawrie, Mirning Elder from the Nullarbor in South Australia and the youngest of five whale lore holders. Bunna lets me know when Gurawul is on the move.

I would also like to acknowledge all the Elders and keepers of the whale story up and down the east and west coast of Australia who shared their knowledge and contributed their stories about the whale as I journeyed around the country.

Thank you to the Gurandji tribal dancers of the Yuin Nation who continue to dance the whale journey on land to hold the lore of Gurawul and to the Gurandji men who went with me to Tasmania to see the engravings.

Thank you to the artists, Wayne Thorpe, Peter Hewitt, Brendan Lugnan and Jeremy Devitt, who painted the Whale Dreaming triptych in March 2021 while on the lore camp.

I would like to thank Magabala Books for providing the research grant that enabled me to journey to Tasmania and visit the site with Julie Gissing, Robyn Swanson, Wayne Thorpe and filmmaker Michael Gissing.

Finally I would like to thank my ghostwriters, Julie Gissing and Robyn Swanson, for helping to capture this story so that people not only hear my words but now they can also read about Gurawul. Putting the words of my Elders into story, they are helping me continue our cultural tradition of storytelling. Thank you for keeping my memories alive.

NOTES

1 Bunna Lawrie is a member and respected Elder of the Mirning Aboriginal tribe from the Coastal Nullabor, South Australia. He is a Mirning whaledreamer and songman, medicine man and storyteller of his tribe.

2 Alison Nannup, *Bindi-Bindi Koondarminy Wer Maamoong Waangka – Butterfly Dreaming and Whale*, Batchelor Press, 2013.

THE AUTHOR

Max Dulumunmun Harrison was a deeply respected and revered Elder of the Yuin Nation, which extends from Wollongong down the east coast of Australia to Gippsland and out to the Southern Tablelands of NSW. Initiated by his grandfather and uncles into the traditional ways when he was a teenager, his great gift was his ability to straddle two cultures, to communicate and share his wisdom and knowledge with Indigenous and non-Indigenous people alike.

Photograph by Pablo Martin

Born in 1936, he grew up moving with his family from camp to camp to escape the dreaded Welfare. He had little formal education and taught himself to read and write. From the age of 10, his grandfather and uncles took him walking with them on country, teaching him how to learn from the land. From these masters he learnt respect and sacredness and connection to the greatest teacher of all, nature.

Over the course of his life, he worked in various occupations, including Aboriginal health services, where he worked tirelessly with those affected by alcohol and other health issues. In recent years his charity Back to Country has helped many young men to discover their culture and identity.

His life's purpose has been to pass on the teachings of his Elders, which he referred to as the 'living treasures' of his life, saying that he had to 'give it away to keep it'. Over the years he has taught students in schools and universities and advised government ministers as well as Australia's leading architects. His first book, *My People's Dreaming*, was published in 2009. In December 2021 he passed into the Dreaming, leaving behind a huge legacy.

THE ILLUSTRATOR

Laura La Rosa is a writer, critic, designer and illustrator. She completed a Bachelor of Creative Arts (Graphic Design), receiving two dean's awards for academic excellence.

Laura is passionate about the entire creative production process. This is the first book Laura has illustrated.

A proud Dharug and Calabrian woman, Laura lives on her ancestral lands, Dharug Country, the land she grew up on.

This book is dedicated to my friend
Emmanuel Fillaudeau and my brother-in-law
Michael Murray.

Whale bone painted by Emmanuel Fillaudeau and group.